ANIMAL RIGHTS

FARM ANIMAL RIGHTS

Jessie Alkire

Checkerboard
Library

An Imprint of Abdo Publishing
abdopublishing.com

abdopublishing.com

Published by Abdo Publishing, a division of ABDO, PO Box 398166, Minneapolis, Minnesota 55439. Copyright © 2018 by Abdo Consulting Group, Inc. International copyrights reserved in all countries. No part of this book may be reproduced in any form without written permission from the publisher. Checkerboard Library™ is a trademark and logo of Abdo Publishing.

Printed in the United States of America, North Mankato, Minnesota
102017
012018

Design: Christa Schneider, Mighty Media, Inc.
Production: Mighty Media, Inc.
Editor: Megan Borgert-Spaniol
Cover Photographs: Shutterstock
Interior Photographs: Alamy, p. 25; AP Images, p. 19; Shutterstock, pp. 4 (left, right), 5, 7, 11, 12, 13, 14, 15, 17, 21, 23, 24, 27, 28 (top, middle, bottom), 29 (left, right); Wikimedia Commons, p. 9

Publisher's Cataloging-in-Publication Data
Names: Alkire, Jessie, author.
Title: Farm animal rights / by Jessie Alkire.
Description: Minneapolis, Minnesota : Abdo Publishing, 2018. | Series: Animal rights | Includes online resources and index.
Identifiers: LCCN 2017944019 | ISBN 9781532112591 (lib.bdg.) | ISBN 9781532150319 (ebook)
Subjects: LCSH: Livestock--Social aspects--Juvenile literature. | Animal rights movement--Juvenile literature. | Animal welfare--Juvenile literature.
Classification: DDC 636.0019--dc23
LC record available at https://lccn.loc.gov/2017944019

CONTENTS

WHAT ARE
FARM ANIMAL RIGHTS?

When was the last time you visited an animal farm? Maybe you did so on a class trip long ago. However, it is likely that farm animals affect your life every day. Farm animals provide humans with food products and many other materials. This includes your burger at lunch and the leather in your shoes!

Meat, dairy, and eggs are the most commonly consumed farm animal products. But farm animals contribute to many non-food items as well. Their fats are used in candles and beauty products. Their skins are used for clothing and shoes.

Today, most farm animals are raised in factory farms. These large indoor farms raise animals as quickly and cheaply as possible. This often results in poor living conditions and **inhumane** treatment of the animals.

Animal rights **advocates** fight for the rights of farm animals. They encourage the public to support more humane farming methods. But can these methods feed a rising global population? New laws, advanced **technology**, and growing support for animal rights will bring big changes in farming!

DOMESTICATING FARM ANIMALS

Before farming, people hunted animals and gathered plants from the wild. The first animals to be **domesticated** for food were sheep. This occurred between 11,000 and 9,000 BCE in Southwest Asia. People used sheep for meat, milk, and wool. Goats, pigs, and cattle were domesticated shortly after.

With these domesticated animals, people had more consistent food sources. They didn't have to travel to find food. They could settle and create permanent communities. Animal domestication also changed the way people related to animals. The animals were no longer wild. Instead, they were considered property.

Farm animal domestication happened much later in the United States. Europeans settled in North America in the late 1400s and

Since animals were first domesticated, farmers have practiced selective breeding. For example, a farmer may only breed cows that produce the most milk.

early 1500s. They brought horses, cattle, sheep, and pigs with them. These livestock provided food and clothing for the settlers. They also pulled heavy farming machinery. Animal farms and ranches began to appear in colonial America.

RISE OF FARMING & INDUSTRIALIZATION

By 1800, 90 percent of Americans lived on farms. These farms were small and run by families that lived on the property. Animals had plenty of space to graze. Their health and well-being were personally managed by the farmers raising them. Farmers produced food for themselves and local markets or butcher shops.

This changed with the rise of the **Industrial Revolution** in the United States. More people moved to cities to work in factories. Farm products needed to be transported farther to reach consumers in **urban** areas.

Farmers started raising more animals to provide enough meat for growing urban populations. Around this time, the first commercial meatpacking plants opened. Farmers sold their livestock to the meatpacking plants. The plants then slaughtered the animals, processed their meat, and sold it to meat markets.

In the 1880s, new **technologies** such as railroads and refrigeration helped the meat industry grow. Meatpacking companies used refrigerated railcars to transport meat to markets across the country. In the 1900s, refrigerated trucks started being used as well.

There were many other machinery advancements in the 1900s. New slicing, grinding, and packaging machines made meatpacking faster and cheaper. Americans continued to consume more meat and pay less for it.

Chicago was the meatpacking center of the nation until the 1920s. The city's Union Stock Yard held animals before they went to slaughter.

FACTORY FARMING & ANTIBIOTICS

The industrialization of farming led to a complete change in agriculture. Demand for meat and other animal products kept rising. The population of the United States was also growing. Companies wanted to make products as **efficiently** as possible. This led to large indoor farming operations called factory farms.

The first factory farms were created in the 1920s and 1930s. They weren't very successful. In a factory farm, more than a thousand animals lived in close quarters. This allowed diseases to spread easily. Many animals got sick and died.

In the late 1940s, veterinarians began to use the antibiotic penicillin on farm animals. This helped prevent the spread of diseases. But researchers discovered another benefit of

More than 100 million pigs are raised and slaughtered in the United States each year. Nearly all of these pigs come from factory farms.

Farm animals usually consume antibiotics in their feed or water. Farmers may also give their animals shots of antibiotics.

antibiotics. These medicines made the animals gain weight faster than usual.

In 1951, the Food and Drug Administration (FDA) approved the use of antibiotics to promote growth in farm animals. By feeding their livestock antibiotics, farmers could send the animals to slaughter sooner. This meant farmers could raise more animals in less time.

In addition to boosting animal growth, antibiotics were cheaper than the proteins farmers had been feeding their animals. By adding antibiotics to their animals' feed, farmers cut costs on production. Antibiotic use became an industry standard in farming.

With the help of antibiotics, factory farming was more successful. The number of factory farms began to rise in the 1960s and 1970s. They needed to meet the demands of a growing population. The factory farming industry has continued to expand worldwide ever since. Today, these large farms produce about 70 percent of the world's meat. They produce 99 percent of the meat in the United States!

FEEDING THE MASSES

The greatest benefit of factory farming is its ability to feed the rising global population. In 1800, there were close to 1 billion people in the world. In 2016, there were 7.4 billion people. Factory farming is the most **efficient** way to produce food for the masses.

Farm animals grow much more quickly in factory farms. The animals consume grains, antibiotics, and **hormones** to grow bigger faster. Chickens grew to about two pounds (1 kg) in 16 weeks in 1920. Today, chickens in factory farms grow to about five pounds (2.3 kg) in seven weeks! Because animals grow faster, factory farms can raise more animals and produce more products.

Factory farms also use machines to do much of the labor. Machines dispense food, milk cows, collect eggs, and more. This speeds up the production process. It also lowers the cost of human labor.

All of these factors help factory farms produce the most food as quickly and cheaply as possible. The increased supply of products and decreased labor costs help keep consumer prices low. However, this **efficiency** comes at great costs. Animals, humans, and the **environment** are all affected by factory farming practices.

Chickens are usually slaughtered when they are about 42 days old.

15

ISSUES & ETHICS

Animal **advocates** believe that factory farming is **unethical**. They protest the **inhumane** conditions that factory farm animals are forced to live in. For example, the animals cannot roam freely and graze on their natural diets. Instead, they live mostly indoors in unclean quarters or cages.

In factory farms, chickens' beaks are often trimmed to keep them from pecking themselves or others. Cows' horns are removed for safety and their tails are cut shorter to make milking cleaner. These practices cause the animals pain and discomfort. Factory farm animals can also grow deformities from antibiotics and **hormones**. Many gain too much weight and can't stand up.

Advocates argue that conditions during transport to slaughter are also inhumane. The animals are packed tightly into trucks for hours without food or water. Then, slaughtering is done as quickly and cheaply as possible. This often results in animal suffering.

Factory farm chickens are kept in battery cages. These small wire cages leave very little room for movement.

Factory farming practices could threaten human health as well. Researchers think antibiotics in animal feed could lead to antibiotic resistance in humans. This means antibiotics would no longer work to treat bacterial **infections** in humans.

Factory farms also produce tons of manure and other waste. The waste often seeps into ground soil and water. This pollution harms animal and human health as well as the **environment**.

THE FARM ANIMAL MOVEMENT

The effects of factory farming have led to a growing movement against the practice. The 1975 book *Animal Liberation* by Peter Singer helped spark this movement. Before this book, many people were not aware of how factory farms were run. *Animal Liberation* exposed factory farming practices to millions of readers. It inspired a shift in attitudes about the treatment of animals.

Around this time, the **vegetarian** movement was also gaining popularity. More people were thinking about the effects of their diets on animals. They were choosing to eat less meat or no meat.

In the 1980s, many groups formed to fight for farm animal rights. Farm **Sanctuary**, the Farm Animal Rights Movement, and **Humane** Farming Association were among them. Groups like these work to raise public awareness of farm animal welfare. They aim to pass laws that improve living conditions for farm animals. They also work to reduce meat consumption nationally and globally.

The 2008 film *Food, Inc.* had a huge influence on the farm animal movement. It further raised awareness of factory farming and animal welfare. Many people joined the movement and changed their diets after seeing the film.

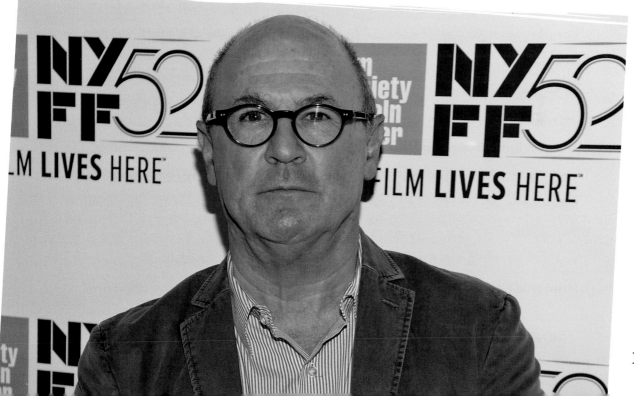

Robert Kenner is the creator of *Food, Inc.* He believes the farm animal movement will change the way we eat in the future.

LAWS & REGULATIONS

One goal of the farm animal movement is to pass stricter laws that protect farm animals. The Animal Welfare Act of 1966 regulates the care of certain animals. But it does not apply to farm animals. And most US states do not include farm animals in state anti-cruelty laws.

One law that concerns farm animals is the Twenty-Eight Hour Law. It was passed in 1873. This law requires trucks transporting farm animals to stop every 28 hours. This is to allow the animals to eat, drink, and exercise. However, the Twenty-Eight Hour Law does not apply to birds.

Another law is the 1958 **Humane** Methods of Livestock Slaughter Act. It says animals must be stunned before they are

Farm animals face distress and possible injury when they are transported. They are often overcrowded and unable to move around or rest.

slaughtered. This practice helps eliminate or lessen animals' pain during slaughter. However, this law does not apply to birds.

Other countries have stricter regulations for farm animal welfare. Animal rights laws in the European Union are based on the Five Freedoms. Among them are freedom from discomfort and freedom to express natural behavior. The European Union has also banned **battery cages** for chickens. Several European countries, including Sweden and Norway, have banned beak trimming.

LOCAL & ORGANIC FARMS

Increased awareness of factory farming **ethics** has inspired many to look for other food sources. One **alternative** is small, local farms. Many of these farms allow their animals to roam outdoors. These farms are also more likely to feed cows their natural diet of grass rather than grains. Small, local farms more closely resemble the family-run farms from before the **Industrial Revolution**.

Organic farms are also gaining popularity. These farms must meet certain requirements to label their meat products as organic. The farm animals must have outdoor access. They must be raised on natural land that is not treated with artificial chemicals. They must also be fed **certified** organic foods. Animals on a certified organic farm cannot be given antibiotics or **hormones**.

Organic farms raise animals in healthier conditions than factory farms do. Organic farms may also be better for human health. Their meat and dairy products do not contain antibiotics that could cause antibiotic resistance in humans. These products also contain more healthy fats that are good for the human heart.

However, these benefits come at a cost. Organic products are much more expensive than factory-farmed meat or dairy products. Many people choose non-organic foods because they cannot afford organic products.

Many people are choosing to raise their own chickens in their backyards. They do so for eggs, meat, or to keep the chickens as pets!

CHANGING TIMES

The rise of organic farming is one of many developments in the farm animal movement. In 2017, the FDA banned the use of antibiotics to promote weight gain in animals. This ban aimed to prevent antibiotic resistance in humans who eat animal meat. Antibiotics can still be used to prevent disease in animals. But now farmers need veterinary approval to give their animals antibiotics.

The farm animal movement has also aided **environmental** efforts. Animal and environment **advocates** push for stricter regulation of waste and pollution from factory farms. Such action is necessary for both human and animal welfare.

In the past thirty years, there has also been a rise in farm animal rescues. Groups such as Farm **Sanctuary** rescue mistreated and neglected farm animals. The animals are moved to sanctuary farms or adopted by loving families.

RIGHTS
SPOTLIGHT

FARM SANCTUARY

Founded in 1986, Farm Sanctuary
is the largest farm animal rescue
organization in the United States.
It works to rescue sick, injured,
and newborn farm animals
from inhumane treatment. The
organization then cares for these
animals in sanctuaries in New York and
California. There, the rescued animals can
roam and graze freely for the rest of their
lives. Farm Sanctuary educates people about
factory farming and offers public tours of its sanctuaries.
It also works to pass a wide range of animal rights laws.

Farm Sanctuary rescues
farm animals from factory
farms, stockyards, and
slaughterhouses.

FUTURE OF FARMING

With rising awareness of animal welfare, experts believe farming changes are in store. The number of local and organic farms is expected to rise in coming years. However, the world's population is still growing. Factory farms may be necessary to meet the growing demand for food and keep costs low.

Researchers are exploring new farming practices that increase production without harming farm animals. Some farm animals now wear sensors that track their health and well-being. This makes it easier for factory farmers to manage large numbers of animals. Such advances could also improve farm animal welfare.

Scientists also continue to explore human diets that do not include meat from farm animals. Some experts argue that

The vegan diet is growing in popularity. This plant-based diet cuts out all animal products, including eggs and dairy.

humans can get all the proteins and energy they need from plants. However, not all experts agree on the benefits of these diets.

Still, more and more people are making decisions that support farm animal welfare. This includes eating less meat and buying from local or organic farms. Meanwhile, advances in **technology** may lead to more **ethical** farming practices. These solutions will shape the future of farming!

TIMELINE

11,000–9000 BCE   Sheep in Southwest Asia are the first animals domesticated for food.

MID-1800s   The Industrial Revolution reaches the United States and the first commercial meatpacking plants open.

1880s   Refrigerated railroad cars allow meatpacking companies to transport meat across the country.

1951   The FDA approves the use of antibiotics to promote animal growth.

1960s–1970s   The number of factory farms rises to meet a growing population and demand for meat.

1986   Farm Sanctuary, the nation's largest farm animal rescue organization, is founded.

2008   The popular film *Food, Inc.* is released. It raises awareness of factory farming and other agriculture issues.

2017   The FDA bans using antibiotics for weight gain in livestock in the United States.

BECOME AN ANIMAL ADVOCATE

Do you want to become an advocate for farm animals? Here are some steps you can take today!

Spread the word. Education is key! Tell your family and friends about farm animal rights.

Buy local. Buy animal products from small, local farms. You'll support both the animals and the farmers running these farms!

Read labels. Read the labels on animal products. Look for information on organic certification, antibiotic use, the animals' diets, and more.

Research organizations. Find an animal rights organization that is right for you. You can become a member, go to events, or sign up for newsletters!

GLOSSARY

advocate – a person who defends or supports a cause.

alternative – a choice from among two or more things.

battery cages – small wire cages arranged in rows. Factory farms use battery cages to house many chickens in limited space.

certified – recognized as having met certain requirements.

domesticate – to adapt something to life with humans.

efficient – wasting little time or energy.

environment – nature and everything in it, such as the land, sea, and air. *Environment* can also refer to surroundings, especially those that affect the growth and well-being of a living thing.

ethics – rules of moral conduct followed by a person or group. Something that is unethical is morally wrong.

hormone – a chemical messenger that helps regulate activities in the body. Certain natural and artificial hormones are given to farm animals to make them grow faster.

humane – kind or gentle to people or animals. Something that is inhumane is lacking kindness.

Industrial Revolution – a period in the mid-1800s in the United States that marked the change from an agricultural to industrial society.

infection – an unhealthy condition caused by something harmful, such as bacteria.

sanctuary – a refuge for wildlife where hunting is illegal.

technology (tehk-NAH-luh-jee) – machinery and equipment developed for practical purposes using scientific principles and engineering.

urban – of or relating to a city.

vegetarian – living on a diet consisting mostly of plant foods and sometimes eggs or dairy products. Vegetarians do not eat meat, poultry, or fish.

ONLINE RESOURCES

Booklinks
NONFICTION
NETWORK
FREE! ONLINE NONFICTION RESOURCES

To learn more about farm animal rights, visit **abdobooklinks.com**. These links are routinely monitored and updated to provide the most current information available.

INDEX